William Hamilton Merritt

John M. Bassett
A. R. Petrie

Date Due

Canada's Father of Transportation

 WELLAND CANAL

150th Anniversary Committee

1829 - 1979

This book, written by two leading Niagara educators, is presented through the courtesy of The Ontario Paper Company Limited to recognize the historic contributions to the Niagara Region and to Canadian transportation by William Hamilton Merritt, George Keefer, and their associates.

Fitzhenry & Whiteside Limited

Contents

© 1974 Fitzhenry & Whiteside Limited
150 Lesmill Road,
Don Mills, Ontario, M3B 2T5

Printed and bound in Canada.

ISBN O-88902-200-3

The Sentry Chapter I

The sentry stood so still that even the squirrels ignored him in their frantic search for food. A pair of cardinals, their scarlet feathers bright even against the autumn leaves, tilted their heads to examine him more closely. The birds decided he was harmless and continued with their meal of seeds and berries.

It was the year 1812. War had broken out between the United States and British North America. The militiamen of those days wore the leather jackets and trousers of the frontiersman. The only thing that showed that this was a soldier was the musket cradled under his arm.

The sentry was keeping his watch on the Niagara River. From his position on the cliff he could see downstream, at the river's mouth, the American Fort Niagara on the west bank, and the Canadian Fort George on the other. On the shores of Lake Ontario, the Newark Lighthouse rose high above any other building in the tiny town.

But a glimpse up river gave an entirely different picture. The mists from Niagara Falls hung high in the sky. Between the falls and the sentry was a wilderness of huge oaks and maples already turned into a blaze of reds, yellows, and browns. Below, at the foot of the cliff, the river creamed white as it raced through the rapids to the lake.

Even after a few short days, the sentry was bored with the war. Standing alone in the bush for hours on end was certainly not a pleasant way to spend the day. There were so many things to do. But, as long as the war lasted, the young man's ideas could not be put into practice. He was a farmer by necessity, a trader by inclination, and a soldier only by accident.

The sentry, however, was unaware of the scene around him. In his imagination, he could see the river below filled with the sails of proud merchantmen, sailing majestically for a thousand miles into the very heart of the continent. Food, furs, and timber would come down the river, passing the manufactured goods going up.

Canada, his new country, could become one of the greatest in the world, if its rich share of nature's wealth were combined with man's industry.

As the sentry looked at the mists of Niagara Falls, he frowned. Nothing bigger than the canoe of an Indian or a voyageur could pass the great falls. But there must be a way. If he could only see the end of this war, he would try to solve the problem.

But the end was nowhere in sight. He sighed. As a member of the militia, he was proud to help defend his country. But there was so much to do back on his farm on Twelve Mile Creek. More than that, he had so many plans: for a store, for factories, for trade up the Niagara River, if he could only find a way around the falls. He must see if he could get permission to go home to harvest the crops.

Bugles from both forts downstream broke his daydreaming. He would soon be relieved of his duty. He stretched, to restore the circulation in his arms and legs. The cardinals flew quickly to cover, and the squirrels scolded him from the safety of the trees.

William Hamilton Merritt, the nineteen-year-old sentry, turned his back on the river and started down the slope to the road below. But the river was never to be far from his thoughts for the next twenty years. Young Merritt had caught the glimpse of a great dream. That dream was somehow to make the Niagara River part of a great transportation system that would open up the centre of the continent.

Once the war was over, the dream was to become a reality in an amazingly short time.

The Journey to Chapter 2
Twelve Mile Creek

Will Merritt, the sentry by the banks of the Niagara River, had not always lived in Canada. In fact, he and his family were fairly recent arrivals. The Merritt family came to Queenston in 1796, when Will was only three years old.

William's father had been a firm Loyalist during the American Revolution, and so Mr. Merritt felt it would be wise to leave his home in New York State and move to Canada.

Will Merritt never forgot the wilderness walk of his family: his mother and father and sister, Carolina. As the family fled to the Canadian border, they found it necessary to avoid the mail roads as much as possible. They travelled only on Indian trails, scarcely marked out in the thick bush. It was not long before the Merritts' legs and arms were scratched and bleeding. But their lives depended on keeping going, no matter how painful it was.

"How far is it to Fort Niagara"? asked Will, as the party stopped to rest.

His father thought for a moment. "We skirted Oswego two days ago, so we must be almost there. Say another three days."

Will slipped down beside his mother. Young as he was, he could see the strain of such a journey on this slight woman. But she smiled at him as she took his hand. "Keep going, Will, we'll soon be there, and then we can have heat and a proper meal and a bed. It won't be long."

But the chill autumn winds that blew without stopping certainly did not add to their comfort.

"We'll have to go a few more miles before we bed down for the night," warned Thomas Merritt, as he shifted his pack and shouldered his musket once more.

Will struggled to his feet. "Can I help you, mother?" he asked. Mrs. Merritt smiled down at him. "Just take my hand, son, and we'll manage."

Dark had settled in by now. It was almost impossible to see the path, although the night was clear, and the moon was well up in the sky. Occasionally shadows loomed across the path, or a stray bat swooped low over the struggling party. But the presence of the friendly Indians who were their guides made them all seem safer.

Now they had entered a dense, evergreen thicket. The sharp odour of pine needles filled the air. "This will make a good spot to bed down for a bit," said Will's father. "But mind, no fire or light. There's still some Indian tribe that wouldn't mind collecting our scalps."

Will was used to the routine. He helped collect cedar boughs, and spread them out for a bed. In a few moments, everyone in the company had done the same thing. It was surprising how comfortable a bed they made. But Mrs. Merritt longed for the soft straw mattresses and the cotton sheets they had enjoyed before their flight from their old home.

Will's father had made a wise guess. Inside of three days they came to the mouth of the Niagara River. Everyone was excited, but none so much as young Will, who dashed down to the river's edge shouting in his happiness. He became quieter when he saw a tear slide down his mother's cheek. What was still an adventure for a small boy, meant the end of a life of comfort for Mrs. Merritt.

But small boys do not spend much time in regretting the past. Fort Niagara caught Will's eye. It was an impressive structure, built of wood. Sentinels kept up their steady pace along the stockade wall. But straggling groups of Loyalists were a common sight in those days, and the sentries did not even bother to challenge them.

Several ships and small vessels lay at anchor off the jetty. Around the walls of the fort were fields of corn, grain, and vegetables. Several Indian longhouses were visible at the edge of the woods, and the smoke from their camp fires rose lazily into the air.

Other Loyalists quickly left the fort and started to question them. "How long have you been on the road? Where do you hail from?" and the inevitable questions,

"Have you any news of my brother/my husband/my son?"

The journey was still not over. Although Fort Niagara appeared to be large enough to hold thousands, the flood of Loyalists fleeing to Canada had already overtaxed its facilities. The very next day the Merritt family, along with their meagre belongings, were bundled into a longboat and transported across the river. Accommodation on this bank was far different from that on the side they had just left. A scattering of miserable huts and lean-tos were the only buildings in what was soon to be the capital of Upper Canada.

Mr. Merritt had no intention of staying there. "Come along, Will, we'll find the land surveyor's tent and see what we can get for a new home." A nod and a smile from his mother, and Will slipped his hand in his father's and off they went.

Neither the surveyor, with a week's growth of beard, nor his quarters were very impressive. On a rough wooden table was spread an equally rough map sketched on thin parchment. Beside it flickered a dirty horn lamp.

"What can I do for you?" demanded the surveyor gruffly.

"I come to claim crown land as a loyal servant of His Majesty," replied Will's father.

How was a settler's land allotment decided?

The surveyor pointed to the map. "There's nothing left closer than ten miles back from Niagara," he said. "Would that interest you?"

Mr. Merritt looked at the map for some minutes. "What river is this?" he asked, pointing to a river that emptied into Lake Ontario.

"We've called it the Twelve, because it's twelve miles along the lake from the mouth of the Niagara."

"Is it a fairly steady flow?" asked Tom Merritt, always very conscious of the necessity of water to the pioneer.

"None steadier," was the reply.

"Then I'll stake my claim for 200 acres there," said Tom. The surveyor wrote his name in the spot that Mr. Merritt indicated. This pencilled name was the only claim Merritt would have to his new farm.

It was one thing to identify a claim on a map, but quite another thing to find it, and stake it out, in a virgin forest. Young Will was aware of the long absences of his father, who tramped up and down the Twelve Mile Creek until

he was certain of his land. He blazed trees at the four corners, and then began to build a temporary hut.

Everyone did what they could, to try to have some sort of shelter before the winter. A permanent home would have to come later. Fortunately, the government supplied rations of corn and salted pork. This food was increased by berries and other wild fruit that Will and his sister helped to pick.

When the first rough hut was built, and Mr. Merritt was able to rest briefly from his labours, Will said to his father, "I think I am going to like it here, father." He looked at the beautiful autumn colours and the fast-flowing stream.

"I'm pleased for you, son," said the elder Merritt, not wishing to destroy this youthful optimism. Neither father nor son could have dreamed of the great changes and contributions that William Hamilton Merritt would make in his new country.

1. Why were the surveys inaccurate?
2. What was parchment? Why was it used for maps and other important papers?
3. What problems did the settler encounter during his first winter?
4. How did the settler become largely independent?
5. How did he make soap, candles, salt, and linsey-woolsey?

A Surveyor's Tent

Chapter 3 **At Sea**

Hard work and determination enabled the Merritt family to establish themselves in their new land. Young Will worked as hard as he could to help his father clear the land and build a good home. But, throughout his life, Will was driven by an urge to try the unknown; to give up the safe and sure for the imaginative and daring.

When he had just turned sixteen years, he sailed as a merchant adventurer aboard one of his uncle's ships, the barquentine, *Lord Sheffield*. Will's uncle had established a successful business, trading down the Atlantic coast. This voyage was to Charleston, in South Carolina. Rich profits, too, were to be made in the trade between Halifax and the West Indies. Will was determined to get these profits. This was to be the first of many disappointments for him.

At first the voyage was uneventful, and the ship sailed south under a warm sun and a steady wind. For William Merritt it was enough excitement to feel the surge of the waves, smell the salt air, and hear the snap of the sails in the lively breeze.

But it was not to last. With Charleston still two days off, a tropical hurricane, born in the Gulf of Mexico, crossed the ship's path. The creaking vessel dipped and rolled, as its bow dug deep into an immense rolling breaker. Spray dashed above the deck, and threw one struggling sailor down. He slithered, cursing, trying to gain his footing, while he clung with all his strength to a line strung across the well.

The storm had broken just as dusk settled over the tossing sea. Even the skipper felt a secret fear. Of all the storms he had weathered, this was the worst.

The helmsman spun the wheel, attempting to keep the bow into the wind, but under the fury of the waves the wheel was almost wrenched from his grasp. The ship's bell sounded, and the helmsman knew his watch would soon be over. Then he could get some relief from the wind and spray with a cup of black coffee-and-rum in the galley.

The *Lord Sheffield* had sailed out of Halifax Harbour ten days previously with a mixed cargo of flour and timber. The flour was in barrels below deck, but the timber was lashed to the deck itself. All aboard could only hope it would not break adrift under the ceaseless pounding of the waves.

Will had said to his uncle, who was on board, "I guess we'll make a fortune when we sail this lot down south, sir."

His uncle had puffed on his pipe for a moment before answering. "There's many a slip, lad, between having and hoping. Our first job is to get this lot safely delivered, and then we'll talk about fortunes."

William Merritt was to attempt many occupations in his life. As part-owner of the cargo on the ship, this was his first venture into making money. In the future, he was to be a storekeeper, miller, distiller, and farmer, but he would never forget his first experience with trade.

Merritt's real destiny lay in the not-too-distant future, but certainly he was not to be an Atlantic trader. As the night passed, the storm grew gradually worse. The darkness blotted out everything. Finally, the mast was smashed. The ship slowly heeled over, and the pumps could not manage to keep the water level down.

The end was not long in coming. The deck cargo shifted and broke loose. Suddenly, the *Lord Sheffield* lurched and, in a twinkling, turned turtle and threw men and equipment, like fleas from a dog's back, into the sea. A few managed to cling to a raft and some of the debris, but the majority of the crew slipped down to their death.

Will was among those hurled into the boiling sea. After what seemed an eternity, his lungs almost bursting, he broke the surface. As the crest of a wave carried him to its height, he spotted a broken spar with a sailor clinging to it. Will had learned to swim well, and it stood him in good stead now. With several powerful strokes he reached, and clung to, the tossing spar.

Will was still spluttering and spitting up sea-water as he wrapped one arm firmly around the spar. His companion was already exhausted and had a bad cut on his forehead. "Are there other survivors?" choked Will.

"I saw some clinging to a raft a few minutes ago," replied the sailor, "but they've since disappeared."

An hour or more passed. Will felt the strength ebbing

out of his numb limbs. The waves buffetted the two men, and tore at their grasp. Will changed arms every so often, and he and the sailor, whose name was George, linked arms in mutual support. George was middle-aged, had spent most of his life at sea, and had survived one previous shipwreck. This experience and encouragement helped Will to cling to life with every bit of his strength.

Another hour passed, which seemed like a century. Suddenly Will thought he saw a faint light glimmering through the wind-blown spray and driving rain. "There's a light," screamed Will.

"Where?" asked George anxiously.

"Fifteen degrees to port!" shouted Will over the crashing surf.

"You're right, lad," confirmed George, and in the same breath shouted "Ahoy!" at the top of his voice. Then they both shouted together, but no one heard their cries. They continued to shout until they were hoarse. But the light of the passing vessel slowly faded from view, driven before the storm. With it faded their hope. Will's heart sank, but George hid his disappointment and, with a voice full of determination, said, "Never mind, lad, there'll be another along soon, and it looks as if dawn is about to break."

Dawn did come, indeed, but it was dull grey with fast-scudding clouds. Gradually the wind died down. But the waves still leapt to meet the sky, and, with every lurch, nearly tore Will loose from the spar. He could no longer move his fingers, and his body felt as if it were a mass of bruises.

When hope was almost gone, and neither of them could mumble a word or scarcely open their eyes, a vision appeared over the horizon. Was it a mirage? No, it was real! It was a square-rigger, with sails furled, but still moving rapidly before the wind.

What are the shrouds, the lanyards, the sheets?

With their last remaining strength they shouted once more. Their voices were feeble and high-pitched. "Ahoy!" "Over here!" "Save us!" Would they be heard? Arms flailed the air in desperation. At last, someone sighted them, and the ship came about.

The vessel bore down on them, threatening them again as the bow split the waves. One blow against the hull and it would all be over. Suddenly, it was on them. So near and yet so far. A line was flung out but slipped through their grasp. They were too weak to cling to the help offered.

As hope grew fainter, Will felt his clothing tighten about his chest, and he was lifted bodily on the end of a pike-pole held by a burly deck-hand. Swiftly, he was swung inboard, and landed heavily in a heap on the heaving deck. At the same moment, George was being hauled over the gunwale by two other hefty sailors. They had made it.

They were soon dressed in warm, ill-fitting, borrowed gear, and seated in the galley over steaming bowls of soup. Will couldn't believe his good fortune, but he was worried about his uncle's fate. The rescue ship had seen no other survivors, but they would soon be in harbour where they could make further inquiries.

As the vessel eased into its moorings alongside the jetty at Charleston, Will leaped ashore and raced for the custom house. A small knot of people was gathered about the door, talking excitedly. They were discussing the big blow and the several ships known to have gone down. But they also talked of some survivors plucked from the sea by a local coaster.

"Where are the survivors?" cried Will, almost in tears. "Over the way at the Crossed Arms," replied the helpful customs officers.

Will fairly leapt across the street and into the arms of his uncle, who emerged at that very moment from the hotel door. "Uncle, you're safe!" cried Will, tears streaming down his cheeks. The ship was gone, but they had survived, and it was enough.

Merritt's hope of a quick profit sank with the ship. "I guess you'll be returning to my brother's backwoods farm in Upper Canada, eh, lad?"

"You're right, uncle. This is too rough a life for me. Losing a fortune in a moment is too risky a way of making a living. Back to the Twelve I'll go, as soon as I can get passage there. It may be the backwoods now, but give us time and we'll turn that land into a fortune."

Storm and Shipwreck

1. Why is this type of sailing vessel called a barquentine?
2. What cargo might such a vessel carry to the West Indies?
3. Will expected to make the trip from Halifax to Charleston in twelve days. To do this, how many miles would the *Lord Sheffield* sail each day?
4. How did the *Lord Sheffield* steer her course? Why was she more helpless in a storm than a merchant ship today?

Store- Chapter 4
Keeping

But the valley of the Twelve to which Will returned was very different from that he had left. It was rapidly becoming settled and developed. Already, there were a dozen mills strung along the stream. These ranged from a distillery to a fanning mill. Salt licks had been discovered and were being worked. Will saw great possibilities and profit to be gained from this valley.

By now a small community had sprung up at the corner of the road, and the valley had been named Shipman's Corner after a local taverner who had set up business there. In due time this village would become the city of St. Catharines.

Will Merritt decided to try his hand at a quieter trade after his lucky escape from the sea. He joined William Chisholm in a general merchandising store, which served the settlers and mill-owners of the district. The store was centrally located and was a meeting place for travellers and settlers alike. One of these early inhabitants was on his way to Will's door at this very moment.

The bell above the door jangled sharply, as a large man, staggering under the burden on his shoulder, lurched into the store. Merritt, alerted by the bell, motioned to the man to put his sack of potatoes next to several barrels piled in the corner.

Will Merritt took his heavy leatherbound ledger from under the counter. With his quill pen he made a credit entry in the account of John Hainer, one of the earliest settlers along the valley of the Twelve. The ledger showed a total credit of £4 10s 6d York currency in Hainer's name.

What methods of trade were used?

While William Chisholm, Merritt's partner in the general store, examined Hainer's produce, John was busily selecting his purchases in exchange for his potatoes. Among these were a bolt of linsey-woolsey produced locally, a half-pound of square iron nails, and two lumps of rough soap.

As Hainer still had credit in his favour, he asked Will for the remainder in money. Will went to his strongbox (for he acted as banker as well as merchant) and selected several varied coins. John checked each coin carefully, biting one or two of those which were chipped or worn. There was an American half-eagle, a Halifax shilling, and a Spanish doubloon, together with several English pennies and halfpennies. Will Merritt, meanwhile, checked their current value in a book recently issued by the printers in York. The value of the coins altered considerably, and their exact worth was always in question.

At that moment, as accounts were being settled, the stagecoach from Queenston rolled noisily to a stop outside the door. Several passengers got down, while the driver unloaded the heavy trunks from atop the coach. All the passengers were covered with a fine film of dust from the short journey, but one figure was unmistakable. He was tall and gaunt, with a weathered and hawk-like face. He walked erect, despite the handicap of his pegleg. It was Ranger John Clement, a well-known fighter with the Confederacy of Indians south of the border.

Ranger John was warmly greeted by Will and Hainer to whom he was well known, despite his infrequent visits to the Twelve. Even the most hardy seldom travelled any distance except by boat, or, if the rivers were frozen, on ice. Not only did such a journey take a long time, but it damaged the rough trails which were called roads.

"What brings you here?" asked Will Merritt, although the sack the traveller dragged through the door gave a strong clue to the answer.

"A new shipment of hatchets, shears, and other hardware just arrived yesterday by schooner from England via Montreal and Kingston," replied Ranger John, as he showed his goods to the eager merchants and several other possible customers who had clustered around. "They are the very best made, and I felt I might barter them for a good price in this area."

He was correct. In a very short time a bargain was struck. Goods of this sort were still rare in the valley of the Twelve and found a ready market. In exchange, Ranger John took ten pounds of salt, a gill of oil, and some paper of lampblack, leaving the remainder as future credit on Will Merritt's books.

This was Merritt's daily routine until he sold his store to someone else in the growing community of Shipman's Corner. Will had an idea. Soon the Twelve would be harnessed for a mill of its own with a steady year-round water supply, and ships docking and being built not far from where this very store stood.

Trading at the Store

1. Would you expect the storekeeper to stock bread and butter? If not, why?
2. What is meant by "cottage industry"?
3. Why was money such a problem to early settlers?
4. What do you identify in this store? What could some of these containers hold?

This bill reproduced below was written in 1810. It suggests a number of aspects of life in those days.

1. What was the kind of currency in use then?
2. What might the "value received" have been?
3. Why did Garret Scram have to make "his mark"?
4. The trustees of St. Catharines Church are asking for "lawful interest"; what interest is charged by a bank today?

Chapter 5 War with the United States

Why did Loyalists settle on the Niagara Frontier?

All during the summer of 1812 rumours of war with the United States spread throughout the small country of Upper Canada. The thought of such a war was horrible to families such as the Merritts. They had left secure homes and businesses so that they could remain peacefully under the British flag. To find that the war was still following them was a cruel blow.

Militia companies were organized throughout the country. Their numbers were pitifully small, and their weapons, except for the family shotgun, did not exist. Troops of the regular army could not be spared from the war in Europe, where the British Army was in a life-and-death struggle with Napoleon.

The wide-ranging Yankee pedlar was one of the principal sources of information. While the Merritt women carefully examined his wares, one of them chatted with Mr. Merritt.

"From what I see, Mr. Merritt, if the Yanks decide to grab off your country, they'll go through here like a hot knife through butter. And a good thing, eh? We're all the same stock here, we're all one, ain't we?"

Mr. Merritt hesitated a moment before answering. "What you say is correct. We're all one, as you say. But I was born in New York State; my son, Will, was born there also. But we left our home, our land, our wealth, because we felt there was something in this country worth working for." He waved at the rough cabin, the few acres of cleared land, and the few cattle. "We think we have here what we were looking for, and I reckon we'll fight for it, if necessary."

Will had been listening to his father with some surprise. The elder Merritt rarely spoke of the past. "There'll be no war here, father. Why, we're so poor that even the Yankee pedlars treat us as charity cases."

The pedlar smiled. "With what I'm letting these cloth goods go for, I'll be a charity case before ye." But, as he continued, the smile disappeared. "Mark my words, Mr. Merritt, there'll be war here before the year is out."

Unhappily, the words of the pedlar proved right. War broke out in the autumn of 1812. However, the pedlar was wrong on another point. Instead of the American Army marching victorious and unopposed through Upper Canada, the British regular troops and the Canadian militia won a series of victories. But victory was expensive. The commander of the British forces, General Brock, was killed at Queenston Heights, as he led the charge that drove the invaders back into the river.

Will Merritt enlisted as soon as war broke out, and by the summer of 1813 he had gained a reputation for courage and intelligence. He was put in charge of a small group of mounted militia. Their duty was to annoy the enemy, make lightning raids, and find the strength and position of the American outposts. Soon Major Merritt and his group became known on both sides of the fighting line. It was dangerous work, but young Merritt found it an exciting challenge.

Life was hard on the settlers. As the fighting moved back and forth across the peninsula, homes were wrecked and provisions stolen. Churches and large houses were turned into hospitals or barracks.

By early summer, the Americans had pushed almost to the western end of Lake Ontario, and were camped at Stoney Creek. The British troops were outnumbered five to one; it seemed certain that the Americans would continue their advance.

A group of ensigns and other junior officers were clustered around a camp fire, wondering what the dawn would bring. "As sure as the sun comes up tomorrow, the Yanks will be at us and we'll keep retreating and retreating, unless . . ."

"Yes, George," put in Major Merritt. "Unless what?"

"Unless we attack them. They'll never expect us to turn and face them. Besides we've got the Indians, and the Yanks are deathly afraid of our Indians."

"George, that makes a lot of sense. Let's see what Colonel Harvey says." The young officers, excited at the thought of ending this steady retreat, flocked to the headquarters tent.

Colonel Harvey agreed with the plan. In a short time 500 men moved under cover of the darkness to the attack. Outnumbered as they were, the only hope of success lay in complete surprise. The American sentries had to be captured without a sound, and Major Merritt and his men successfully carried out this vital mission.

Finally, General Vincent gave the order to charge. A tremendous shout split the silence of the early morning. Mixed with the wild yells of the Indians, the sound would have made a brave man run. The hillside was lit up with musketry fire. A few groups held out, but the surprise had been so complete that the bulk of the American Army turned and fled.

The battlefield was almost deserted when Colonel Harvey sent for Merritt. "Merritt, I fear that General Vincent has been taken prisoner. See what you can find out. But be careful. Don't take any foolish chances."

Merritt turned, and rode his horse through the battleground, which was littered with the wreckage of war. After the furious fight, there was a strange silence. Perhaps Will was thinking too much about the battle; in any case, before he could move, he saw a musket pointed at his chest. It was held by a sturdy American soldier.

Merritt drew in his reins. He was about to surrender, when he thought he might as well try to bluff his way out. The heavy, blue coat that Merritt wore could just as easily have been the uniform of an American officer.

"Who ordered you to stand there, soldier? And don't point that gun at me. It might go off. Your troops are halfway to the border. After them now, before you get into more trouble."

The soldier scarcely knew what to do. "I was told to stand guard here, sir."

"Yes. Well, I'm telling you to join your outfit. Off with you now."

The soldier turned and ran. Merritt chuckled to himself as he continued his search.

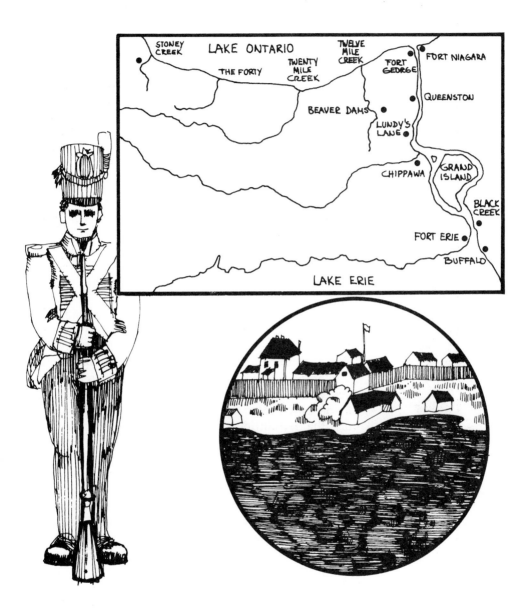

1. How many flags flew over Fort Niagara? Why?
2. Whose flag would be flying over Fort Niagara in this picture? How would it differ from today's?
3. The soldier has a flintlock musket. How does it differ from a rifle?
4. Why are today's uniforms more suitable for battle?

The Niagara Frontier

Chapter 6 The Battle of Lundy's Lane

The war continued into the summer of 1814. Both sides gained victories, both suffered defeats. Both heartily wished the fighting would end. To make life even more miserable, the summer of 1814 was the hottest in living memory. The small fields that survived the marching armies dried up under the merciless sun.

A regular soldier of the War of 1812

But it was the regular army soldier who suffered most. Military regulations forced the soldier to wear his woollen uniform and to be properly dressed at all times. This meant wearing the tunic buttoned up to the neck. Wearing a full pack on sentry duty under the blazing sun, choked by the dust, tortured by mosquitoes, the ordinary soldier somehow managed to keep his determination and pride. But although he grumbled— and envied the militiaman leaning in the shade— he knew quite well the task that lay ahead. If the Yankee was to be driven from Canadian soil, it was he— the regular— who would have to do it.

In the small town of The Twelve, William Merritt had found a shady spot in the doorway of St. George's Church. It was a poor building, but had been taken over by the army as a hospital. Will glanced inside and was happy to see that it was completely empty. He could not know that, within twenty-four hours, it would be crammed with the victims of the fiercest battle of the war so far.

The war seemed far away. Merritt wanted to get on with the building of stores, taverns, factories; the frontier needed so much. But he knew that his dreams would have to wait. The village of St. David's had been burnt to the ground, so now an American town would have to be burnt in revenge.

Deep in his dreams, Merritt stepped into the road almost under the hooves of a galloping horse. Only the

skill of the rider saved him from being unseated. He
swore as he reined his horse in.

Streams of sweat creased the dust-caked face of the
rider. "Watch out, Major. And tell me where Colonel
Scott is. It is urgent!"

Merritt pointed out the headquarters. The rider spurred his horse forward, jumped down, and strode past the
sentry at the door.

Within minutes, everyone in town, soldier and
civilian, had heard the news. The British and American
forces were locked in a fierce battle near Niagara Falls.
Colonel Scott was to bring every available man, regular
and militia, to stop the American advance.

"I do hear they've twenty thousand men up there,"
said a farm lad as he checked his gun.

His friend looked around at the few hundred men
who were swiftly forming into line. "You be dreaming,
boy. There ain't that many men in the whole Continental
Army. Let's get going, I say. I've me cows to milk when
we've tidied this lot of Yankees away."

Bugles and shouted orders rang out. Horses were
saddled. In minutes the long line had formed and was
moving off to battle, ten miles away. The regulars
marched well, and their proud bearing gave everyone
confidence.

The militia, for their part, were clothed in every kind
of imaginable dress. Bringing up the rear, was a small
group of men armed only with hunting guns or scythes.
Many a lad in his teens, starting so bravely to war, would
never return.

Colonel Scott called his officers around him as they
moved off. "The enemy has attacked General Drummond just above Niagara Falls. It's a full-scale attack this
time. The General says that if the Americans are not
stopped here, they'll take the whole peninsula. It's up to
us to get there quickly to lend a hand."

As he spurred forward, he called out, "Merritt, over
here. The messenger says they're fighting in a cemetery.
Where the devil's that?"

"Almost ten miles straight ahead, sir. If we follow this
road, we'll come out on a hill that overlooks the cemetery." Before Merritt had finished, the Colonel spurred
his horse to the front of the column.

As the day went on, the heat grew more and more

unbearable. Jackets were dropped by the side of the road, but no one slackened pace. The miles quickly disappeared. Everyone seemed aware that this was to be one of the vital battles of the war, that even such a small detachment as this might make the difference between defeat and victory.

Finally, toward late afternoon, the sound of firing could be heard in the distance. Colonel Scott brought the column to a halt and waved his officers to join him. "It sounds as though General Drummond may be in need of us, so, gentlemen, we shall push right on. Make sure your men are supplied with ammunition." He gave their orders to the officers.

To Merritt, he said, "Get to the top of the hill near the cemetery. You may be able to cause a diversion, if you come on the Yanks from the rear. Make all the noise you can when you attack. Carry on, then."

Merritt saluted and turned to his small detachment. "You heard the Colonel, men. Let's see if we can do what he wants. Don't get separated; don't fire till I give the word; and go as quietly as you can till we see them."

The hill was barely twenty feet high, but the thick underbrush made movement difficult. Suddenly, the leading soldier held his hand up. Merritt moved silently to his side. He could scarcely believe their good fortune. There, at the top of the hill, was a battery of two cannon and only ten blue-uniformed Americans. Their backs were turned to Merritt, as they kept up a steady fire on the British troops below.

Merritt beckoned his men around him. Silently, they moved into position to wipe out the small gun-crew. But, this time, Merritt's good luck deserted him.

Fierce screams split the air. Down the hill from the rear poured a troop of Indians loyal to the Americans. The Canadians were caught between two forces, and the fighting became confused. Merritt fired at the yelling Indians, but a huge orange ball seemed to explode in his face. Before he fainted, he saw a tomahawk raised above his head, but he was unable to move.

It was pitch-black when Merritt recovered his senses. Wave after wave of pain flooded through his head. Carefully, he raised his hand to the back of it. He could feel blood caked there, but did not appear to have suffered any other injury. The firing had stopped, so the battle must be over.

He managed to sit up. At first his eyes had difficulty in focusing. Finally he saw that he was by a fire, with someone watching him from the other side.

Will tried to speak. "Is it all over? Did we stop the Yanks?"

The man on the other side of the fire burst out laughing. "It's all over, all right. All over for you. You'll be spending the rest of the war in a prison stockade."

Will looked around. He could make out the blue uniforms of the American soldiers. He never knew how he had got there. His head continued to pound, and the American soldier continued laughing. "It's all over for you, me lad. Lundy's Lane they call this excuse for a road, but for you, lad, it's the end of the road."

Chapter 7 The Road Back

Will was on the road back! Shortly after the end of the war, an exchange of prisoners had been arranged, and Will was among those released.

His clothes were shabby and worn and certainly wouldn't have passed a military inspection, but he'd managed to get a new pair of boots from his captors and a few dollars from friends in the States. But money and his appearance weren't the most important things in his mind. His thoughts were far away as he strode along, a cloud of dust rising in his wake.

There was no turning back now. His mind was made up. He would marry Catherine, his sweetheart, as he had said he would many times during his service and his imprisonment.

Will thought of some fond memories, as he made his way north at a steady pace. When he had first met her seemed long ago, yet he remembered the day so vividly that it might have been yesterday.

What are corduroy roads?

He'd been fishing in the Twelve, as was his custom, and had caught some healthy bass and trout which were plentiful there. Suddenly, he heard a carriage rattling down the rough road which led from the escarpment. It sounded as though it was going too fast to get safely round the sharp curves, and excited voices shouting at the horses strengthened this fear. Then it came! A grinding crash of splintered timber and the frightened neighing of horses.

Will dropped his fishing pole and catch, and raced in the direction of the crash. As he cleared the woods, he could see through the settling cloud of dust a buckled wheel and the splintered cab door hanging from one hinge.

Will wrenched the door open and peered inside. "Anyone hurt?" he shouted. The passengers were all in a heap. A girl's voice answered weakly, "I don't think badly, but please help my mother. I think she's fainted!" This was Will's first meeting with his wife-to-be.

Together with the driver, Will helped lift Mrs. Prendergast down. She soon came round, and the family were able to find out the extent of their injuries. Fortunately, except for a few bruises and scrapes, they were all sound. Dr. Prendergast, Catherine's father, was quite capable of attending to these minor injuries.

Will stayed by until everybody had been looked after. In the course of the treatment of a bruise on Catherine's leg, he could not help noticing the pretty ankle and calf. It was at this point that Will blurted out, "You must stay at our place until you are able to build a home of your own. We have plenty of room."

"That's very kind of you, my lad," rumbled the doctor. "You're sure it won't be an inconvenience?"

"Ah, not at all," insisted Will.

And so it was agreed, and Will raced off to get a wagon to carry their belongings to the Merritt household. "Wasn't that kind and considerate?" Catherine said to her mother. She, in her turn, had not been unaware of the handsome face of their young helper, and was delighted with what had happened.

Once they were comfortably settled into their quarters, the conversation about the young man continued, with growing enthusiasm on the part of Catherine and her mother. "I'm well pleased that we are to have such fine neighbours," beamed Mrs. Prendergast. "They seem refined and well-bred."

And so what had begun well grew in intensity over the next several years. Feelings grew deeper as Catherine and Will matured. There was a dark cloud on the horizon, however. Things were so troubled and unsettled, because of the chances of war, that Dr. Prendergast felt the family should return to the more settled existence of Mayville, New York. There, too, he had considerable prestige as an influential member of the state legislature.

Thus it was that Will had had to suffer separation from his beloved. As the war had grown closer, even the mails, always uncertain, were cut off completely. During the war he had heard almost nothing of Catherine and her family. But, contrary to many people's experience, Will's love had not cooled. Now he was heading back and he could hardly wait to hold Catherine in his arms once more.

Miles had passed while Will had been daydreaming, and now a signpost came into sight announcing:

MAYVILLE. Will hailed the first citizen he saw. "Where's Doctor Prendergast's house?" he enquired.

"Two blocks down this street. It's the large white house on the hill with the picket fence around it. You can't miss it," said the helpful stranger, pointing the way.

Scarcely had Will pushed through the gate when he was seen. Catherine rushed into his outstretched arms. They smothered each other with kisses, and Will held her so tightly that Catherine could scarcely breathe. Yet she didn't want him to let her go. When she finally caught her breath, she sobbed, "Oh, Will, I've missed you so!"

"Not half as much as I've missed you," said Will, equally moved, "but it's over now, and we will never again be separated!"

True to his word, Will became formally engaged, and the wedding took place on March 13, 1815. The marriage had the warm support of both families who had long hoped for this event.

It was a gala affair—as weddings were in those days—an occasion for a gathering from miles around. Former enemies mingled freely in the happiness of the occasion.

"Aren't they a handsome couple?" chirped the matron of honour. "Perfectly matched," replied the best man. Another toast was proposed, and then the dancing began. Will led his bride on to the floor, and all soon joined in. They danced waltzes and schottisches to the music of the four-piece orchestra, which had been brought in from the capital for the occasion. And so it went on into the small hours of the morning.

At last the happy couple were allowed to escape, but not until the carriage, which the neighbours had decorated with ribbons and bows, had been dragged by the young men down the lane to their new home. Then followed the chivaree, when everyone circled the house, banging on all kinds of metal pots and pans, and firing muskets wildly into the air.

After a few days' honeymoon, Will and Catherine said good-bye to the Prendergasts and made their way on horseback to The Twelve, via Buffalo and Black Rock. Needless to say, a warm welcome awaited them at their old homestead.

"All happiness to ye," shouted one old neighbour as

they passed his gate. "See you both at the party tonight," declared another. "There's a whole series of celebrations, with the grand one at Colonel Clark's in two weeks' time," giggled a third.

"It looks as if our honeymoon will last at least a month, Catherine, my love," smiled Will, "and our happiness will last a lifetime." Catherine nodded and smiled shyly. She would never be more beautiful nor radiantly happy than at this moment.

The Wrecked Carriage

1. What sort of roads would the Prendergast family have travelled over? Were accidents common?
2. Was it easier to travel in summer or winter?
3. A *brougham*, a *clarence* and a *victoria* are all private carriages named after people. Do you know who these people were? Would you expect a victoria to be used when Will and Catherine were married?

The Miller Chapter 8

Will stood gazing at his extensive holding along the valley of the Twelve. This was very different from the first small homestead he and Catherine had lived in shortly after their wedding.

The spring breakup was in full swing now, and the white, swirling waters and chunks of sharp ice tumbled with a subdued roar into the valley. These rushing waters at the same time turned the water wheels on the mills lining the creek.

By 1818, there were a dozen such mills above and below the falls. Benjamin Canby had built one of the earliest grist mills in this area, but after a few years had sold out to the Honourable Robert Merritt. His executors, in turn, had sold it to John of the famous Street family of millers. Will Merritt had soon built another mill below the mountain for grinding grain.

Several rough wagons were lined up to unload their grain for grinding into coarse flour at Merritt's mill. The wooden mill wheels, constructed so carefully, creaked as *How were mill wheels made?* they turned, and the great round stones crushed the kernels between their surfaces.

Further west, out of sight, Will had constructed and operated at various times a sawmill, a salt factory, a potash factory, and a distillery.

These mills were located in the gravel left behind by a retreating glacier ages before. They were called the Short Hills. The mills there produced necessities for a growing community. Lumber was needed for homes, stores, and outbuildings. Salt was used to preserve meat and other perishable food when the icehouse ran out. Potash was used in making crude soap from animal fat; and whisky from the distillery, at twenty-five cents a gallon, was always welcome at barn-raisings or other bees.

The salt was obtained from salt licks or little rivers, which occurred naturally in Louth. It was extracted by a simple boiling process. Lieutenant-Governor Simcoe, himself, had encouraged its production, and Merritt had invested in one such mill. The Reverend Robert Addison of Niagara controlled the other in the region of the Twelve.

Will turned his gaze upstream. At the top, he could see John De Cou's oil mill. Before DeCou had built his mill, flax seed had been a useless by-product in the manufacture of linen thread. This, when woven with wool, produced "linsey-woolsey," a rough cloth used for making clothes. Now the flax seed was another important item of income for Will's neighbours.

DeCou, helped by Colonel Hamilton of Queenston, had imported the necessary machinery from Scotland for the construction of this oil mill. He had also run a highly successful sawmill since 1792.

These enterprises were very fortunate. During the recent war with the States, the mills along the Niagara River had been plundered and pulled down. By contrast, these mills along the Twelve had led a protected existence and suffered little or no damage. But while they enjoyed this advantage, their distance from big settlements and their lack of good transportation were distinct disadvantages.

Will hoped to put all this right. His father had already dreamed of a canal which would join the valley of the Twelve with Chippawa Creek. Not only would this waterway provide cheap and ready transport for goods, but it would ensure a steady, year-round supply of water for his mills, and for those of his fellow mill-owners.

Already there were rumours of an American canal, the Erie, which would go around the Niagara Falls, and make the Portage Road from Queenston to Chippawa unnecessary.

Will felt his route up the valley of the Twelve would be of more advantage than the proposed Erie Canal. Furthermore, he must preserve the flow of trade through Upper Canada to the west, if they did not want to lose the British connection which they had so lately fought for.

All these thoughts raced through Will's dreaming mind like the water through his sluices, as he sat, soothed by the roar of the waterfall, and sucking contentedly on his long pipe packed with plug tobacco.

C.W.JEFFERYS

1. How many kinds of mills can you think of? Is there a mill that does not grind anything?
2. How far would the settler have to come to Will Merritt's mill?
3. Why did he come in winter?
4. Why did he use oxen and sleigh?
5. What power was used at the mills? What other power might have been used?

At the Grist Mill

Chapter 9 A Canal to By-Pass Niagara

George Keefer

1. *Keefer was of Huguenot ancestry. Why did the Huguenots leave France?*
2. *What other engineering projects did the Keefers take part in?*

Storekeeper, miller, salt miner, journalist: William Merritt always found some new occupation to interest him. Will was always on the lookout for a challenge, and a challenge came only a few years after the war was over.

It all started when Merritt's friend, George Keefer, stormed into his store. Keefer's face was angry. He was so upset that, for a moment, he could not speak. He stood there waving in Merritt's amused face what looked like a legal document.

"Have you seen this, Will?" Keefer continued waving the paper at Will. "We're in a proper fix now."

"Sit down and stop waving your arms around. You look as though you had lost your last penny. Now, sit there and tell me what's up."

"Everything's up. Maybe you're right. Maybe each of us has lost his last penny. A lot those precious politicians in York care. They'll see us bankrupt."

"Oh, come, George. Your crops are in. Why, you told me yourself that it's the best year since you started farming here."

"What good's a crop if you can't sell it? And that's exactly what this piece of paper is all about. See, here is the Governor's signature and he forbids me, you, every man jack of us, from shipping our corn to the States. We either ship it to England, and lose everything in shipping charges, or we let it rot. Either way we lose everything, but I'd rather see it rot than be told what to do at every step."

Merritt sat down opposite his friend. He put two glasses on a small keg and carefully filled each to the brim. "Drink this, George, and then we'll talk."

Keefer started to speak, but Will Merritt held up his hand. "Drink first. Then we'll talk."

George Keefer looked at Merritt and started to smile. He raised his glass as though in a toast, and then drank slowly.

Merritt was the first to break the silence. "First, you can't blame the Governor for this. He's only following orders from London. And I know that if we ship through Montreal, the corn has to be loaded and unloaded so often to get around the rapids, that we'd never make a penny."

"Will, we'd have been a sight further ahead if we'd let the Yanks beat us a few years back. Then we'd ship our wheat down the Erie Canal and sell it in New York."

"You don't mean that, George. That's really nonsense. But you've put your finger right on the answer. If the Yanks can do it, why so can we."

"What in tarnation are you talking about? If the Yanks do what?"

Will pulled a map from under the counter and quickly spread it out. "See this, George? Well, what is it?"

"It's a map, of course. Of the Great Lakes and the St. Lawrence."

"Exactly." Merritt put his finger on Lake Superior. "Now, what's to stop a boat going from here to here?" He swiftly traced the route from Lake Superior, through the other lakes, down the Niagara, and out to Montreal and the ocean.

"You're a dreamer, Will. You know what's stopping that sort of commerce. Rapids here and here and here." Keefer jabbed a forefinger at the map and, with a particularly violent jab, pointed at the last obstacle. "And the Niagara Falls. That's all that's stopping your boat from here to here."

"You're right. I am a dreamer. I've been dreaming of these canals ever since the war. But why can't we build canals? The Yanks built the Erie from Buffalo to New York. If they can do it, why can't we?"

"Go on, Will. Let's hear more."

"We start here. We can put a series of locks up the side of the escarpment, and bring all that timber down to the east. They can build canals around the rapids on the St. Lawrence. Why, in five years we could have ships from Europe sailing into the heart of the continent."

No one could long resist Merritt's enthusiasm. "Will," said Keefer, "you've got something there. If it can be done, it will be the making of this part of the world. But where do we start? What do we do first?"

Merritt paused briefly. "George, this is where you and your friends come in. It's up to you and your friends to raise the money. Thousands, no, millions of pounds will be needed. That's the first job and, in some ways, the most important."

Merritt proved to be right. There were many engineering problems, and the skill of the builders found a solution to each. But the problem of raising the money was one that was never really solved.

Friends around The Twelve did all that they could. This was nowhere near enough. Merritt himself went deeply into debt. His father even sold his farm and gave the money to Will.

At last, Merritt realized the government and the international bankers were the only source of sufficient money. In the end, he was forced to turn to them for capital

Welland Ship Canal - Excavation & Blasting at Lower Entrance to Lock 1, looking S. Aug. 26.14.

This is the menu for the dinner to celebrate the hundredth birthday of the Welland Canal in 1924.

— SCOT'S HOSPITALITY —

"Some hae meat and cannae eat an' some hae nane
that want it—but we hae meat an' we can eat
sae let the Lord be thankit."

Menu

··········

HAGGIS

Oyster and Crabmeat Cocktail

Celery and Olives

SCOTS BARLEY BROTH
and Cockieleekie Soup

FINNAN HADDIE

BUBBLYJOCKS AND MOUNTAIN GOAT
and Cranberry Sauce

Chappit Tatties

Hielan' Sproots

Dumplings, Barnesdale Sauce

Apples   Raisins   Nuts   Fruits

Goudie Cheese and

Bannocks and Oatcakes

Scots Shortbread

Tea and Coffee

---

1. Choose a menu for the 150th anniversary in 1974.
2. What might the menu have been in 1824 at the meeting in the Black Horse Inn that launched the Canal Company?

Chapter 10 **Building the Canal**

Merritt's enthusiasm never failed; he was able to persuade enough of his friends to invest in the Welland Canal Company, so that construction could begin. George Keefer, president of the company, turned the first shovelful of earth on November 30, 1824. The snow of an early winter lay upon the ground as a small group of men began work on one of the seven wonders of the modern world.

In spite of Merritt's energy and confidence, not everyone agreed with him. Some wanted a different route. For them, it was a personal matter; they wished the canal to go through their town or their land. Others just laughed at the idea. For this group, regular visits to the canal site meant a steady source of amusement. How was a boat to be raised 300 feet up the side of an almost sheer escarpment?

Others felt that the tremendous job could not possibly be done with the tools available. Pickaxes and shovels were all that the men had to carve the canal out of the earth; the labourers' muscle was the only source of power.

Nature, too, seemed anxious to threaten the work. Where the ground was easy to dig, landslides frequently occurred. Where the earth was difficult to move, the workers found themselves faced with granite ridges.

However, the solid granite of the escarpment slowly yielded to the strength of the men. The cleverness of one of the foremen solved the problem of landslides, and slowly the thirty-five locks up the escarpment took shape.

Merritt was fond of pointing out to visitors, "It's not just that we are opening up trade to the top of the escarpment. We're opening up a seaway 2,500 miles long."

But there was one other problem that could not be solved by all the engineering skill in the world. That was the question of money. Even before the first shovelful of dirt had been turned at Allanburg, raising enough money had been a difficulty.

Merritt himself always seemed to be on the verge of bankruptcy. He put up every cent that he owned. When that was not enough, he sold the various businesses that he had started, which were just beginning to show a good profit. If Catherine Merritt objected to the constant drain on the family money, we do not know. Certainly, she must have been a source of strength to Will.

Merritt's wife, his father, and friends had faith in his great dream. His friends, too, sold property to get the money necessary for such a huge undertaking. But this part of the world was still frontier land, and money was scarce. It was too much to think that such an undertaking could be managed by individuals. Finally, the government of Upper Canada was convinced that the building of the canal was essential to the growth of the province. They granted the infant company $200,000.

What at first seemed a fortune was soon gone. Merritt realized that the money must come from outside of Canada. England seemed the most likely place to find it. So he went to England. On his way he managed to raise a sum in New York City.

His reception in London was at first most unpleasant. Constant delays forced him to stay far longer than he had originally intended. But his toughness eventually paid off, and he was able to write to his friend, George Keefer, that he had raised over $600,000.

But problems were to continue right to the end. In the summer of 1829, when the canal was almost finished, the foreman, Robin Robert, came to Merritt's office.

Two other famous canals are the Suez Canal and the Panama Canal. Read about these canals to discover the problems that other canal builders experienced.

Merritt looked up from his papers as the foreman entered the room. "You look as though you'd lost your last dollar, Robin. What in heaven's name is the trouble?"

Robin paused before replying, "Sometimes I think we'll never open the canal, Mr. Merritt. If it's not one thing, it's another. No matter what we do, we can't keep the water level up in the locks."

Will shrugged his shoulders. "You're right, Robin. There's always something, and somehow a person never gets used to it. You say the water level won't keep up. Why?"

"It's the locks that aren't holding the water, I reckon. Oh, we can't blame the carpenters. I think the wood was not properly seasoned, and the joints are splitting when the water gets on them."

"I'm sure you're right, Robin. And we can't blame anybody. If only we'd had more time, we could have done a different job. No use complaining now, though; hire the carpenters again, Robin. They'll do the job, even if they have to rebuild every gate."

"Aye, Mr. Merritt. They'll do a fine job, but, begging your pardon, Mr. Merritt, has the company got the money to pay them? The men won't lift a hammer unless they're sure the money's there."

"Money. Always money. But who can blame them? They have families to feed." Merritt paused, and then turned to his foreman with a smile. "We've finished all the digging, haven't we?"

"That we have Mr. Merritt."

"So we've got shovels, pickaxes, wagons, horses?"

"That we have, Mr. Merritt."

"Well, sell it all, Robin. Sell the whole works. We don't need any of that stuff now, and with the money it brings we'll be able to put the carpenters to work. They'll have those locks fixed before freeze-up."

This was not the last of the many problems that the builders had experienced. Illness came. Cholera swept through the ranks of the labourers, and for a time threatened to stop work completely. Again, a granite ridge at Port Robinson would have stopped less determined men. Landslides occurred with annoying regularity, and all the time, over every other consideration, was the need for money.

But problems can be solved. Before the end of the year 1829, the canal was ready to lift a ship through its 35 locks up the Niagara Escarpment, 327 feet high.

The artist has drawn a picture here that illustrates how the early canals worked.

First Welland Canal—Lock at St. Catharines

1. Can you explain how the lock gates were closed and opened?
2. Why were horses necessary in running the canal?
3. Each lockmaster was given a handsome house quite close to his lock. Why would such a house be necessary in the early days of the canal?

Chapter 11 Niagara Falls Conquered

One misfortune after another threatened the success of the canal. In the fall of 1829, when the canal seemed ready, an early and very heavy snowstorm marked the beginning of winter. The cold weather and the violence of the storms delayed the filling of the canal from the Grand River. The feeder line, only two feet wide and four feet deep, barely supplied enough water to fill the locks at the best of times. With the line plugged by ice and snow, the flow of water was hopelessly slow.

The president and directors of the canal agreed that this was no time to open it. "No use wrecking what we've got by rushing. We can wait till next spring. The Falls will still be there and the canal, too, we hope."

But waiting did not appeal to Will. He knew that the enemies of the canal would sneer at the delay in opening it up. Possibly they might do more than that. Feelings ran high in those days, and, to make matters worse, the Canal Company had got mixed up in the violent politics of the times.

But the morning of Thursday, November 26, dawned bright and clear. The sun shone and the snow began to melt.

"Mrs. Merritt," said Will, "I do believe we are going to have some good luck yet. If we can find a captain that's willing, we'll take his boat up the side of the escarpment before the week's out."

Two schooners had just that day anchored in Port Dalhousie Harbour, the Lake Ontario entrance to the canal. They were the *R. H. Boughton* of Youngstown, New York, and the *Ann and Jane* of York.

The *Ann and Jane* was a splendid sight. Flags flew from the masthead, streamers fluttered from the arms, and a huge banner inscribed in gold letters the words **THE KING, GOD BLESS HIM**.

Word spread around quickly, and soon the entire

population was out on the banks to wish the two schooners good luck.

Captain Voller of the *Ann and Jane* called across to Mr. Merritt. "What's it to be? We sailed here thinking to use the canal and now we hear it's closed. Maybe you never intended it to be open." It was easy to understand the Captain's anger. His cargo, meant for the upper lakes, might well be useless by spring.

Mr. Merritt paused a moment before answering. The directors had said that the canal was not to open; Will was not even a director, but he was the company's agent. Then, quickly, he announced his decision.

"Captain Voller, you came to sail on the canal, and, by heaven, you shall. But first I'd be obliged to you if you would give me passage on your schooner."

Entrance to Welland Canal—Port Colborne

He jumped from the dock to the deck of the *Ann and Jane*. The crowd roared its approval. The horses for each boat were quickly hitched, and they slowly began to tow the schooners, with the Canadian boat in the lead.

It was, of course, necessary to go slowly on this first trip. They waited until Saturday to attempt the climb up the escarpment. Everything went like clockwork, and by evening both boats had scaled the 300-foot barrier.

They thought that the trip to Buffalo would be made quickly. However, the cold returned and jammed the locks with ice. Captain Voller and Mr. Merritt looked at each other and nodded. "We chop the ice out or spend the winter on the edge of the escarpment. Let's get to it, Mr. Merritt."

The crews of both schooners joined in, and the slow job of chipping away the ice began.

"Captain," Mr. Merritt said at length, "I think we need the help of your crew at the gate."

The Captain nodded and twelve sturdy men jumped to the dock to swing the lock gate open. For a minute nothing happened; but as they heaved together, the gate slowly started moving and finally burst wide open.

"My compliments to your men, Captain," said Will, and the horses once again started along the tow-path.

It was by no means clear sailing even yet. Ice was still a danger, and the debris, floating logs, and branches, left by the workmen, had to be cleared away.

Finally, they ran aground on a ridge of rock and were forced to wait the entire day. But these delays were of minor importance.

On the Monday, Will Merritt wrote to his wife: "On the whole we have been successful and I have tested to my satisfaction that a vessel will pass on the canal in twenty-four hours."

It is interesting to note that a Canadian ship and an American ship opened the canal. Today these two great countries still freely sail the canal together, though Will Merritt would never recognize the present canal.

The two pictures below were taken on the second Welland Canal.

Two masted schooner and small craft are towed through the canal by this small steam tug. Photo circa 1890 at Port Dalhousie.

Remains of original lock gate at Port Dalhousie constructed before 1845.

1. What are the most important changes that you can see from the first Welland Canal?
2. What are the differences shown between the second Welland Canal and the present Welland Ship Canal?

Canals in Canada

On the opposite page are diagrams of the four Welland Canals.

1. There are many canals in all parts of Canada. If there is one near you, or one that you might have seen, draw a diagram to show how it differs from these.
2. Plans are drawn for a fifth Welland Canal. How do you think it will differ from the present one?

THE FOUR WELLAND CANALS
DIAGRAMMATIC COMPARISONS

FIRST WELLAND CANAL
STARTED 1824 —— COMPLETED 1829

TYPICAL VESSEL
LENGTH 100 FT – CARGO CAPACITY 165 TONS

TYPICAL LOCK

LENGTH BETWEEN GATES . . . . .110 FT.
WIDTH OF LOCK . . . . 22 FT.
DEPTH OF WATER OVER SILLS . . . . . . 8 FT.
SINGLE LIFTS . . . . .6 FT. . TO. 11 FT.
NUMBER OF LOCKS 39

SECOND WELLAND CANAL
STARTED 1842 —— COMPLETED 1845

TYPICAL VESSEL
LENGTH 140 FT – CARGO CAPACITY 750 TONS

TYPICAL LOCK

LENGTH BETWEEN GATES . . . . 150 FT.
WIDTH OF LOCK . . . . 26 FT. 6 IN.
DEPTH OF WATER OVER SILLS . . . . . . 9 FT.
SINGLE LIFTS . . . . . 9 FT. 6 IN. TO 14 FT. 3 IN.
NUMBER OF LOCKS 27

THIRD WELLAND CANAL
STARTED 1875 —— COMPLETED 1887

TYPICAL VESSEL
LENGTH 255 FT – CARGO CAPACITY 2700 TONS

TYPICAL LOCK

LENGTH BETWEEN GATES . . . . . .270 FT.
WIDTH OF LOCK . . . . 45 FT.
DEPTH OF WATER OVER SILLS . . . . . 14 FT.
SINGLE LIFTS . . . . 12 FT. TO 16 FT.
NUMBER OF LOCKS 26

WELLAND SHIP CANAL
STARTED 1913 —— COMPLETED 1932-33

LENGTH BETWEEN INNER GATES ___ 859 FT
WIDTH OF LOCK _ _ _ _ _ _ _ _ _ _ 80 FT
DEPTH OF WATER OVER SILLS _ _ _ _ 30 FT. (REACHES 25 FT.)

SINGLE LIFTS _ _ _ _ _ _ _ _ _ _ _ _ _ .46 FT. 6 IN.
NUMBER OF LOCKS _ INCLUDING 3 TWIN _ _ _ _ 8
TOTAL LOCKAGE _ _ _ _ _ _ _ _ _ _ _ _ 325 FT. 6 IN.

THE GUARD LOCK AT HUMBERSTONE IS 1380 FT LONG BETWEEN INNER GATES

TYPICAL LOCK

TYPICAL VESSEL
MAXIMUM LENGTH 820 FT. & CARGO CAPACITY 25000 TONS AT 24 FT. DRAFT.

Chapter 12 A Son's Adventure

Will Merritt was a man who created action wherever he went or whatever he did. This ability to be at the heart of things, when events were moving quickly, was inherited by one of his sons.

In 1837, Merritt's son, also called William Hamilton Merritt, was a student at Upper Canada College in Toronto.

This newspaper, The Welland Canal *was printed for only one week by William Lyon Mackenzie, a bitter enemy of William Merritt.*

1. Why has the extract from the letter of Chief Justice Robinson been printed at the top of the page?

The political situation in that city had moved from bad to worse as the year wore on. William Lyon Mackenzie, leader of the reformers, continued his struggle with the Governor, Sir Francis Bond Head, and the other political parties. Both sides were rushing to disaster; it was only a question of time before some incident would cause actual fighting.

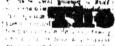

The Welland Canal.
A WEEKLY JOURNAL,

Mr. W. L. MACKENZIE, Member of the House of Assembly of Upper Canada, and Director of the Welland Canal Company.

"If the Welland Canal now gives a return of £4,000, to doubt whether it will in a few years pay £25,000, is no more reasonable than to doubt whether a Calf, if it lives, can ever become a Cow."—*Extract of a Letter addressed by Chief Justice Robinson to Mr. President Merritt, dated Toronto, December 18th, 1834.*

No. 2.   **TORONTO, WEDNESDAY, DECEMBER 28 1835.**   **Gratis.**

Young Merritt had seen Mackenzie only once, but that was enough to give the boy a feeling of dread. Perhaps he was afraid because he knew that Mackenzie had bitterly opposed the building of the canal by his father and many of Mr. Merritt's friends.

Finally, in December, Mackenzie moved on York with a mob of armed men. It was open rebellion.

The headmaster of Upper Canada College had never had to deal with a rebellion before. Because he did not know what to do, he declared a holiday for the students. Merritt, with some of his friends, went to the town centre to see the troops gathering; to hear the exciting rumours; and to feel that they were in the middle of some great event.

Cannon lined the streets in front of the Government Buildings. Soldiers dashed around on very important business. It was all most exciting, and young Will was caught up in the excitement.

"Let's see if we can do something for the Governor," suggested Will. "We don't want to go back to College when there's a chance to do something."

"That's all very well, Will; but how do we get to see someone who can enlist us?"

"Just follow me. We'll see someone, never fear."

And they did see someone. Will strode through the entrance to Government House, his friends following closely. A few questions were asked, a few answers given, and the boys found themselves facing the Governor himself.

"Pray, what can I do for you, gentlemen?" asked the Governor.

Merritt introduced himself and his friends and explained that they wanted to serve against the rebels in some capacity.

Sir Francis coughed, and hesitated for a moment. "Well, yes. Very good of you young gentlemen to offer. We'll certainly keep you in mind. Yes, no doubt we shall need you in a few days. In the meantime, mustn't go hungry, eh?" The Governor turned to his aide. "See the boys are well fed. Now, gentlemen, if you will excuse me."

After emptying a huge plate of tarts and cakes, the boys split up. Most went back to the College, but Will, his brother, and another friend from St. Catharines, decided to head north to see if they could find out anything about the rebels.

As they got to the tollgate that marked the northern limits of Toronto, they suddenly realized that everything was very quiet. There was not another person in sight.

"Let's get out of here in a hurry," said Will, but, as the boys turned to go, they found that it was too late. A number of men, dressed in an odd assortment of clothes and carrying a mixture of weapons, surrounded them.

"What are you young rips up to?" shouted the leader.

Merritt gulped. "We're on our way to school, sir," he said.

"No schools up here. You're a miserable liar and perhaps a spy, too. You know what we do with spies, don't you?" The leader turned to one of his men. "Lock them up. I want to speak to them."

The boys were herded into the little shanty that stood beside the tollgate. The door shut, a heavy lock clicked, and the boys found themselves prisoners.

The younger Merritt tried to keep a quiver out of his voice. "Do you think they'll shoot us, Will?"

"Not a chance. But we'd better see what we can do about getting out of here. See if there is anyone watching us."

"No. Nobody. I think they've all ridden off."

"Good. Help me wedge this pole in the plank." The three boys pulled on the pole. In an instant, part of the shanty wall had been torn off, and they found themselves free.

"I think we'd better get back to College right away," said Will. The others agreed. Keeping down in the underbrush, the boys made their way back.

Somehow, the story of the capture and escape spread. As it spread, it became more and more exaggerated.

"We were pretty stupid to get caught in the first place," said Will. "We were lucky to escape so easily in the second place."

Will's father nodded in agreement. "In the third place, your mother and I are happy to see you both safe and well, but after this leave the fighting to the soldiers."

For his part, Mr. Merritt did not get involved in the fighting, which lasted only a short time. He did his service by sending boatloads of food to Toronto. This helped the people there until life returned to normal.

Iron Horse Chapter 13

A shrill-pitched whistle and the distinct chugging of a labouring steam engine could be plainly heard. "Faith, here comes another load o' ties," cried Mike, the construction worker. He hurriedly scooped another shovelful of gravel under the recently laid iron rails.

The engine was making its way up the steep incline of "The Mountain" at Thorold, on the partially completed Welland Railway. The railway was to take the place of the canal when it was frozen fast in the winter.

How would a railway help build a canal?

"The boss is riding in the engine," said Pat, an Irish immigrant, as he spotted Will Merritt peering from the cab. Pat was one of the many recently arrived Irishmen who lived in "Slab Town," or Welland City, as it was now called. They provided the cheap labour needed during this age of railway-building.

Will Merritt swung down from the cab to see what had been done since he had been there the week before. "Are you checking that gauge frequently?" inquired Merritt of his section foreman, Shean O'Casey, who was built like a bear and swore like a trooper.

"Ye damned right we are, Mr. Merritt!" he replied. "She's six feet apart all the way."

Unlike most railroad-builders, Merritt had chosen to build broad gauge (five foot six), rather than the normal four foot eight.

Merritt moved on down the right of way, examining the region through which they had to push the railway. At this level, the escarpment was formed of shale and some red sandstone, but above was solid limestone, called dolomite, ten feet thick. "We'll need plenty of black powder to blast our way through this," murmured Will Merritt to Bill Donovan, the project engineer, who was trailing behind him.

"We've plenty over in that powder shack," Bill replied. "See, they're hauling it over now to pour down the holes the 'gandy dancers' have drilled."

It was true they had made good progress. But there was a chill in the autumn air which announced the end of good weather for construction. Soon the snow would fly, and it would no longer be possible to bring the rails up by barge on the nearby canal. Furthermore, there had been a delay in the delivery of the iron rails from Britain. It was doubtful if the present supply could keep them busy for much longer, even if the good weather lasted.

"If those rails don't arrive soon," complained Will, "we'll have to lay off some of the men. You know how troublesome they can be when they're idle."

"Yer right," rumbled Bill Donovan, remembering the incident on last July 12. There had been a fight between the Orangemen and the Catholic Irish. It had ended without broken heads only because Father Lynch had drawn a line in the dust of the road with his toe, and threatened to excommunicate any of his faithful who dared cross the line. "We certainly don't want that," agreed Bill.

Satisfied with the progress so far, Merritt and Bill Donovan climbed aboard the wheezing locomotive. The ties had been unloaded from the flatcars, and lay scattered along both sides of the line. With another shrill scream, the engine announced its departure, and backed slowly down the grade on its return to Port Dalhousie for another load.

This was only one of several railway projects which occupied the interest and the time of William Hamilton Merritt in the 1840s and 1850s. Although originally known as a "canal man," Merritt saw the value of the railways. He said that the day would come when his canal and railway would cause St. Johns and Effingham to decline as busy mill centres. Then new communities, such as St. Catharines, Welland City, Thorold, and Merrittville, would boom.

Merritt was also interested in the Intercolonial Line, and when the first company failed he was quick to join with Francis Hinks and others to organize the Grand Trunk Company. "We must borrow money from the Imperial government at low interest, and push the project forward without delay, particularly the portion from Niagara to Detroit," Will told everyone. "When it's completed immigrants and merchandise could be transported from Quebec to Chicago in ten days," he continued. A gasp of disbelief arose from his eager audience. But, then again, if Will said it, it must be possible, for he had done fantastic things before.

But, for the present, the Welland Railway occupied his time and attention. Even so, he had another interest in a line from Niagara to Detroit. This would branch off at a convenient point near Burford, and go on to Hamilton and Burford.

In 1851, two years were to pass before even this short line would be completed. "We'll need plenty of money, hard work, and some good fortune to complete her on time," shouted Will Merritt over the roar of the engine. Bill Donovan nodded his head in solemn agreement, as he watched the work gangs fade into the distance.

Building the Canal

1. When were locomotives first developed? Can you name the inventor?
2. Where did the first railway in Canada run?
3. What route would a canal likely follow? Find the route of the First Welland Canals and later canals.
4. What did the first trains look like? Was it all fun for the passengers?

*The Honorable
William Hamilton Merritt.
Photograph of Merritt in his 60's*

Chapter 14 The Great Span

A great roar went up from the crowd as eager hands on the far shore reached up and hauled down the kite. "You can see it clearly through this glass, Will," said his partner, Samuel Zimmerman, handing Merritt his telescope.

"A long-time dream has now become real," replied Will Merritt, as he looked at the scene on the American side.

His canal-building days well behind him, William Hamilton Merritt had eagerly turned to other interests: first the railways, and now this bridge across the Niagara Gorge. There had been an earlier bridge here, but it had fallen down several years before during a fierce storm. Since then there had been no rail link possible.

Now the first step had been successfully completed. The thin line attached to the kite would haul longer and larger cables across the gorge, until a new suspension bridge was complete. But much work needed to be done before that would happen.

What methods might modern engineers use to put a cable across a gorge?

"Come on, Will, let's have a drink at Forsyth's to celebrate," said Zimmerman. All within earshot took this as an invitation to join them. Glasses clinked, and happy conversation carried on well into the late evening.

At last Will rose and, clasping Zimmerman by the shoulder, he wished him good night, and added, "A project well begun, Sam, and one which will serve us and the Canadas well in the future." His words were to come true.

Months passed, and progress seemed impossibly slow. Stone masons were brought from Scotland to build the two massive stone towers from which the suspension cables were to be hung. The cables themselves were brought in huge coils on flatcars by the Great Western Railway, the railway which the bridge would eventually serve. It was a gigantic piece of engineering, unlike anything undertaken before.

Will met frequently with his partners and those financing the bridge. There was Samuel Zimmerman, whose bank, chartered by Act of Parliament, largely put up the money for the project. There was Keefer, of the famous Thorold family of engineers, who had shared with Merritt the building of the canal; and John Roebling of New Jersey, an American engineer.

They often met at Crysler's "Prospect House" at Niagara Falls, a pleasant and convenient place to do business. (The house still exists.) Here Will had a chance to put forward his ideas about canals and railways. "They are a natural link between existing canals and waterways," declared Will, "and, at the same time, the Grand Trunk and its extensions, the Great Western and the Welland Railways, link our far-flung colonies in British North America."

"You sound like John A. Macdonald, Will," said Sam. "That's what he wants. At the same time, it will keep the trade for Canada, and give us an open port on the sea," he continued.

"I used to think you opposed railways and favoured only canals, Will," chimed in Keefer. "But now I realize they are not enemies, but partners. The canals can carry the bulky produce, while the lighter, more valuable goods can travel by rail."

Suspension Bridge

1. *What problems exist in running a railroad across a long span?*
2. *In what ways are the present "arch bridges" better than suspension bridges? What are their disadvantages?*

"You've got it," agreed Will, as he raised his tankard once more to his lips and drank deeply.

At last the great day arrived in 1855, when the bridge was complete. Military bands and a holiday crowd were present for the occasion. The towers were hung with flags in patriotic colours, and a Union Jack flew from the highest point.

As the last strains of "God Save the Queen" faded, a snorting, wood-burning engine, with a flaring funnel, began to cross on the upper deck. A flurry of sparks and black smoke belched from the stack as it inched across, pulling several cars filled with important people. It was a most impressive sight.

At the same time, on the lower deck, a stagecoach drawn by four white horses made its way from the opposite shore bearing the Governor of New York State and several notable railway and government officials.

"This is a great day for you, Will Merritt," declared Sam Zimmerman. Little did he realize that in a scant two years he'd die on this same line on another bridge when it collapsed while the train was crossing—the Desjardins Canal just outside Hamilton. But nothing spoiled this joyous celebration, and Will accepted the praises of his fellows with justifiable pride and a sense of accomplishment. It was indeed a great day, another in the long line of Merritt's successes.

1. How could a kite carry a cable over a gorge?
2. What conditions in a gorge are particularly suitable for a kite?
3. What steps in bridge-building would follow, once the cable was in place?
4. What is this kind of bridge called? What other kinds are there?

Cable
Over the Gorge

Chapter 15 The Father of Canadian Transportation

HONORABLE WILLIAM HAMILTON MERRITT

In 1862, William Hamilton Merritt died. It seems fitting that his death should take place, aboard a ship, while he was visiting one of the canals that had meant so much in his life. Merritt had been inspecting the canal at Cornwall. True to his nature, he was planning to make the canals even bigger and better, in order to fit them into his dream of a great St. Lawrence Seaway system.

In terms of property, money, or wealth of any sort, Merritt died poor. If this were the only way to judge a man, Merritt might be considered a failure. But, of course, a far better way to judge a man is to examine his achievements. By this measure, few, if any, Canadians could be termed more successful.

When the child, Will, came to the banks of the Twelve, the country was a wilderness. When he died, the banks of Twelve Mile Creek boasted a prosperous, thriving town: St. Catharines. Not all the credit can be given to Merritt, but certainly his energy in opening a series of factories showed others what could be done in this rich area.

We have seen that Merritt served his country in war, as well as in peace. Perhaps the life of Canada depended on the existence of militiamen like Merritt.

But William Hamilton Merritt's greatest achievement was the building of the first Welland Canal. If Merritt had not thought of the idea and completed it in spite of every kind of difficulty, the canal would certainly not have been built. Without the Welland Canal, Canada would be a different place today. Merritt opened up half a continent to trade. Few men can be said to have done as much.

Merritt served his country well in Parliament. He was first elected at Haldimand in 1832, and afterwards was elected seven times as Member for Lincoln. While in Parliament, he spoke on canals in the rest of the country. The Rideau Canal, the locks at Sault Ste. Marie, and the canals on the St. Lawrence owe much to the energy with which he promoted them.

Merritt had hoped to build a railway from Niagara to Detroit. He failed in this plan, and had to be content with the much shorter Welland Railroad. The line he wanted has, of course, long since been built.

Merritt also helped to bridge the Niagara River.

Today, a statue of William Hamilton Merritt stands in a small park in St. Catharines overlooking the site of the first Welland Canal.

It is the statue of a man who served Canada well.

WILLIAM H. MERRITT 1793-1862

Born in Bedford, New York, Merritt came to Upper Canada with his family in 1796 where his father, a Loyalist, acquired land near here on Twelve Mile Creek. During the War of 1812 Merritt served with the 2nd Lincoln Militia. Returning here after the conflict he became a successful merchant and mill-owner. Primarily responsible for the construction of the first Welland Canal 1824-29 he represented Haldimand in Upper Canada's legislature 1832-41 and Lincoln in the Legislative Assembly of Canada 1841-60. He served as Canada's commissioner of public works 1850-51. A strong proponent of improved canals on the St. Lawrence, Merritt promoted many important projects in the field of transportation.

Erected by the Ontario Archaeological and Historic Sites Board.

Credits

The Authors

Mr. John M. Bassett is Consultant for Communications, and Mr. A. Roy Petrie is Superintendent for Operations, at the Lincoln County Board of Education.

The publishers wish to acknowledge with gratitude the following who have given their permission to use copyrighted illustrations in this book:

The Canadian War Museum, National Museum of Man, page 22;
Gordon Dingman, Publishers, Niagara Falls, Canada, pages 45, 60 and 61;
Imperial Oil Limited, page 33;
The Public Archives of Canada, pages 43 and 55.

Every effort has been made to credit all sources correctly. The author and publishers will welcome any information that will allow them to correct any errors and omissions.

Editing: Laura Damania
Design: Jack Steiner
Illustration: Brant Cowie

The Canadians

Consulting Editor: Roderick Stewart
Editor-in-Chief: Robert Read